CRITICISM AND CENSORSHIP

CRITICISM
AND
CENSORSHIP

BY

WALTER KERR

NEW YORK HERALD TRIBUNE

Reviewed in.
Am. Eccl. Rev., p. 9.
When?

1954

CO-SPONSORED BY THE NATIONAL CATHOLIC EDUCATIONAL
ASSOCIATION AND TRINITY COLLEGE,
WASHINGTON, D. C.

THE BRUCE PUBLISHING COMPANY • MILWAUKEE

FOREWORD

The fifth Gabriel Richard Lecture was delivered at Trinity College in 1954 by Mr. Walter Kerr, dramatic critic of the *Herald Tribune,* New York City. For Mr. Kerr it was a return to a familiar neighborhood, since he had spent many pleasant and profitable years just across the street as a leading light in the School of Speech and Drama at the Catholic University.

Mr. Kerr was born in Evanston, Illinois, and after basic work in speech at Northwestern University, where he took his Master's degree, joined the staff of the School of Speech and Drama at the Catholic University of America as associate professor. He is one of the founders of the Catholic University Theatre and has been a director in the professional theatre of such productions as "Sing Out, Sweet Land," "Touch and Go," and "King of Hearts."

Mr. Kerr's specialty has been the theory of drama, criticism, analysis, and, as mentioned above, the direction of productions, along with an outstanding interest in the history of the theatre.

This present volume, *Criticism and Censorship,* is typical of the fine scholarship that has characterized the work of Mr. Kerr over the years. It is a happy addition to the library of books that now make up the Gabriel Richard Lectures.

FREDERICK G. HOCHWALT

Secretary General
National Catholic Educational Association

CRITICISM AND CENSORSHIP

CRITICISM AND CENSORSHIP

1

AT THE MOMENT it does not look as though there were ever going to be any meeting of minds, or any agreement on a community of interests, between the critic who is passionately devoted to the arts and the censor who is worried about the possible indiscretions of the arts.

The two have not only agreed to disagree in our time, they have just about decided never again to speak to one another. The critic has come to the firm conclusion that the censor's role is wholly invalid. The censor is convinced that the critic, in his fanatical insistence on freedom for the arts, is a woolly-headed irresponsible whose attitudes and arguments may be safely dismissed.

The battle is an old one. Plato was half of a mind to outlaw the artist from his ideal society, and his shadow has fallen — in one way or another — on almost every era since. If St. Thomas Aquinas felt that "play acting" was "necessary," there have been a dozen Tertullians or St. John Chrysostoms to question the proposition. Molière might be successful enough to earn the friendship of his King; he could never be successful enough to keep partisans of the cloth from closing "Tartuffe." The Puritans once shuttered every theater in London for eighteen years; the men who reopened some of them immediately produced the most licentious body of comedy England has ever known, as if to even the score. The continuing contest does not really need to be detailed.

One thing might be said about it, to distinguish it from our own disagreement. In most — not all — of the clashes of the past, there was some expectation that the conflict was going to go on till doomsday. Victories on one side or the other were generally thought of as temporary; the playwright who had succeeded in getting a license for one troublesome work did not suppose that this would automatically guarantee him immunity for his next one; the censor who had succeeded in removing from circulation a certain libidinous work did not suppose that other writers would take warning and thereafter refrain from producing libidinous works. Each party to the quarrel felt a certain resignation about the folly of the other — a resignation that went hand in hand with a readiness to fight. The struggle to make art pure, or to keep art free, would rage on forever; someday the rightness or wrongness of each individual battle would come out in the wash; the best one could do was to fight the individual battle.

2

It is this last attitude that we seem to have altered. We have lost our resignation, our willingness to concede that the other fellow's foolishness will probably hound us to the end of time; we mean — right now — to put an end to that foolishness once and for all. We may also have become weary of being ready to fight; we are willing to expend all the energy necessary on one great last battle, provided that we can make it the definitive battle, and that there will be no more skirmishes ever after. We are — on both sides of the fence — resolutely moving in for the kill.

Thus in the field of criticism there is no longer any satisfaction to be taken in getting *Ulysses* through the United States mails, or in securing a license for any single motion picture in any single American city. What must be discredited and defeated is not the isolated instance of unjustified censorship, but the principle of censorship itself. Censorship — *all* censorship, of whatever origin and whatever limited intent — must be seen as an essential violation of fundamental human freedoms, impermissible under any circumstances. Nor is it enough to establish a mental climate, to make the world *see* censorship in this light; the matter must be taken to law, all censorial statutes must be removed from the lawbooks, the courts must make certain that none can be enacted in future. The effort here is not to convince the censor of the error of his ways, but to strip him of the power to pursue those ways. The censor is to be permanently silenced.

Within the past few years we have seen the American Civil Liberties Union, which has fought many a necessary isolated battle, establish a committee to oppose censorship as such. We have seen the editorial pages of the responsible metropolitan press achieve virtual unanimity of opinion in the case of the New York State's banning of the films "La Ronde" and "The Miracle." (Most such opinion held not only that these films should be licensed but that the right of the State to censor by means of licensing should be permanently restricted.) When Bosley Crowther, the film critic of the New York *Times,* takes a lively interest in a current contretemps, he works from the premise — if I do not misinterpret him — that legal censorship is wrong and that taste must be trained to do what the government cannot be permitted to do. The intellectual climate is, in fact, so perfectly crystallized by this time that a critic taking a whack at the ethical standards informing a given piece of work must quickly insert the disclaimer that he does not favor censorship, much as a man attacking certain outrages against our civil liberties feels that he must slip in the information that he is not a Communist. A writer examining the novels of Mickey Spillane for the *Saturday Review* recently

4

concluded that these best-selling thrillers were constructed about the notions that the end justifies the means, that the due processes of law are generally ineffectual, and that recourse to irrational violence is an acceptable means of dealing with evil. He gave the impression of being appalled by his discoveries; but he was careful to add that he would "not be in favor of censoring" the materials. If the critical camp is aware of its literary problem children, it is convinced that censorship is under no circumstances a legitimate means of dealing with them.

On the other side of the fence, the forces favoring censorship no longer seem the least bit interested in contending with the critic; they are out to circumvent him, and his legal ways, altogether. Aware that they are steadily losing ground in the courts, censorial forces have turned away from the courts and toward the formation of powerful pressure groups whose weapons are not so much philosophic or legal as economic. Let the critic claim that he is defending freedom of speech; let the judges of the land decide that the critic is right; there is still a way to render the argument irrelevant and the decisions impotent — keep the customer "voluntarily" away from the market. Neither the critic nor the courts can compel an unwilling spectator to go to a questionable entertainment; the thing to do, then, is to make the spectator unwilling. When — by whatever private or institutional means — enough spectators have been made unwilling, the producers of entertainment will forget all about their victories at law and will begin to appease the reformers, willy-nilly. No producer is going to listen to a critic who loses him money.

Nor are the censorial bodies content with the establishment of a *de facto* control of moviegoing, say, on a bread-and-butter basis. Like the critics who are trying to write *finis* to the quarrel by making further quarrels legally impossible, censors are trying to end the contest — in their favor — by seeing to it that no future controversy, or future chance of defeat, ever comes up. The *coup de grâce* here is a practice that is coming to be known as pre-censorship. That is to say, the producer of entertainment is persuaded — by the same threat of economic reprisal — to subscribe "voluntarily" to a generalized code affecting both the content of his product and the treatment of that content *before* the product is made. Since the producer's acquiescence is voluntary, no legal charge of unwarranted violation of rights can be brought against anybody. Since content and treatment are washed and wrung out in advance, no subsequent battle is likely to develop over the completed work. (The critic may deride it for its saccharinity, but since it is now too late to change anything his outcry may be dismissed as a tantrum.) The battle has been won because

6

the battle has been anticipated — and not fought.

Of course, those tantrums will continue. Critics will go on pointing out that much — perhaps most — of the work done under an established code is immature and unlifelike. Sometimes, glaring sternly at the oversimplifications of human behavior that any code is likely to produce, they will even call it immoral. To make certain that the alerted public is not swayed by any of this rhetoric, the most energetic censorial bodies of our time engage in a continuing campaign to discredit criticism — as such. The man who is principally concerned with the integrity of the arts becomes, in the terminology of the pro-censor camp, a pitiable "artsakist." Prejudicial words are hurled into the fray; the critic is — in effect — condemned as an "aesthete" before he has managed to open his mouth; the term "aesthetic" becomes as much a red flag to the faithful as the term "censorship" does to the opposition. There also grows up in vast areas of the public mind a sense that these two words describe intrinsically unalterable positions, mutually exclusive beliefs. No man who holds with censorship dares dally with the study of aesthetics; no man who is deeply attached to the arts dares consider for a moment the possibility of limiting their circulation. A line is drawn that must not be crossed — from either side.

2

THE TENSION BETWEEN these two irreconcilable factions is especially strongly marked in present-day American Catholicism. Indeed, it sometimes seems as though the struggle over censorship were a struggle between Catholicism and the rest of America, or at least that part of America that is thought of as rigorously "secular." This is, as it happens, quite a false picture; the most important legal battles that have been fought in our time were over statutes on state lawbooks rather than religious principle; and within Catholicism itself there is a sharp running exchange over the nature, rights, and necessity of the arts. But there are reasons why "Catholic" and "censorship" are words that leap to the mind as natural twins.

In the first place, the Catholic is — and is known to be — committed to the principle that censorship is, under certain circumstances, a valid practice. He is a member of a hierarchical institution to which he owes a filial duty; he has paid that duty over the long years by observing the prohibitions of the Catholic Index. He has not found this especially inhibiting; most of the works proscribed are of a highly specialized nature; if he has had legitimate need of them, in the course of his own professional work, he has been given permission to go to them. But he does acknowledge the right of a duly constituted authority to act authoritatively, even in his own chosen field; and the fact serves as a base both for his quite proper identification with the principle of censorship and his quite improper identification with any or all of its aberrations.

The trouble with this identification is that it tends to become total, both in the mind of the Catholic himself and in the mind of the secular citizen who is staring at the Catholic from a distance. The secular thinker, knowing that the Catholic submits to censorship within his own Church, assumes that the Catholic is eager to defend and encourage censorship in all its forms everywhere, that he must be innately sympathetic to the practice of proscription. And the Catholic, especially at a time when the issue is being stated in such emphatic *either-or* terms, vaguely wonders whether he oughtn't to be so oriented. Should a battle over a given work arise, he may find himself thoroughly sympathetic to the critical, rather than the censorial, position; fearing, however, to compromise a principle with which he is in part identified, he may suppress his sympathies and remain a silent and isolated onlooker. He may do more than that. He may brush aside the claims of the defenders of art and put his weight behind every manifestation of the censorial spirit, convinced that he is supporting a general value even when he is guilty of particular error.

The stronger the critical voice against censorship becomes, the more intensely does the Catholic feel his isolation — he seems to be the only man in the world who still believes that certain forms of censorship are defensible. The average parochial Catholic — who may never have been exposed to any discussion of the arts as arts, but who has certainly been exposed to the idea of censorship — makes his first contact with secular criticism in the form of a quarrel. He may never have heard of a certain critic until he finds that critic attacking him, or seeming to attack a practice of his Church. He bristles on acquaintance, reads him — if he reads him at all — with an eye for his error rather than an eye for his argument, and rapidly labels him as an apologist for license. He distrusts this secular critic because he is patently antagonistic; he also distrusts him simply because he is secular. Most good criticism now being written *is* secular criticism; but the Catholic is already alarmed about the intensely secular spirit of the modern world, the progressive divorce of moral value from every other kind of value. The Catholic knows that *he* cares about the moral law; the critic does not sound as though he did. Put together the facts that the critic is very vocal in his opposition to censorship, and that he does not write as though he even knew the difficulties which sometimes give rise to a need for censorship, and a mental picture of this critic forms all too quickly; he is a monster who is insensitive to the actuality of sin and indifferent to the possible effects of sin upon the general health of the community. The Catholic retires into a kind of spiritual fortress, and arms it; the voice making such a racket beneath the windows is the voice of the enemy.

Even the Catholic who finds himself extremely interested in the arts exhibits great self-consciousness as he sets about his work. Let us say that a man is going to be doing some book reviewing for a Catholic magazine. He does not feel free to review a novel on its aesthetic merits alone; that would smack of secularism, and would overlook the fact that his editor and perhaps the majority of his readers are expecting a few remarks on the possible harmful or beneficial effects of the work. Nor is he content simply to make these last remarks, to confine himself to a kind of ethical estimate; he himself is at least as much interested in the pleasure a work may give as in the peril or profit that may attach to it.

To resolve the tension that hangs over him — the tension between the claims of criticism and the qualms of a conscience that accepts censorship in principle — he invents a double standard of judgment. He separates the work into moral and aesthetic elements, and considers these independently. He also gives to one of the isolated elements a clear priority.

A recent review of a novel in a Catholic magazine began, characteristically, as follows: "There are two levels on which a novel may be judged: one, as a piece of writing; two, as a reflection of the morality of the author or the age in which he is writing."

Given this beginning, it was possible to foresee — quite accurately — the whole shape and the final balance of the review. The writer would go on to say that as a piece of literature the novel was first-rate. (There might be a faintly defensive overtone in this, as though the reviewer were acknowledging the merits of the work only because those merits had been so strenuously insisted upon by secular critics.) He would then approach his major qualification; either the "morality of the author" or the general morality "of the age" had so permeated the underlying structure of the work — its sympathies and bland assumptions — that its probable effect upon the reader would be a damaging one. The final verdict: no.

Thus a work of fine art has been accepted as a work of fine art; it has been simultaneously rejected as a vehicle of good, perhaps fiercely condemned as an actual vehicle of evil. Of the two opinions given, the moral takes precedence over the literary. Beauty and truth *are* separable in a work, according to this method; a novel may be beautiful and still be false to the nature of man.

12

When the Catholic turns to criticism, then, he does not content himself with forming an aesthetic evaluation of the object at hand. He feels an additional obligation to make a guess — he hopes it will be an informed one — about the work's subsequent influence on the behavior of the reader. More than that. He tells the reader whether or not he ought to read it. He thus assumes, above and beyond his role as critic, the role of censor. He is, in effect, critic and censor rolled into one — and, at the last, it is in his role of censor that he hands down his verdict.

So long as this double standard — with the nonaesthetic standard carrying the greatest weight — continues to guide the writing of criticism by Catholics, secular critics are unlikely to do more than sniff at the spectacle. To the secular critic the "Catholic critic" does not seem a critic at all — for the obvious reason that he surrenders his function as critic the moment he is called upon to form a judgment.

And it is equally difficult, under these circumstances, for the Catholic to understand his secular cousin. The man who steadfastly refuses to speak of a work as though it had an ethical substructure, or who does not take account of this substructure when making his recommendations, strikes the Catholic as a man who has arbitrarily excluded from his vision of life a sizable portion of that life as it is actually lived. The secular critic

13

thinks the Catholic critic is making prejudicial decisions. The Catholic critic thinks the secular critic is making incomplete decisions. The two stare at one another, baffled.

The distance between these two men is not a theoretical distance, noticeable only in the intellectual stratosphere. It is an operating distance that separates them in the regular conduct of daily affairs. Any secular magazine with a large circulation would, for instance, think twice about taking on a Catholic as a book, theater, or movie critic. A magazine that did accept a Catholic in such a role a year or so ago recently called the critic in and told him, in effect:

"Frankly, we were terribly worried about putting a Catholic in this job. But it's worked out very well — you don't write like a Catholic at all."

I have been reviewing plays for a metropolitan newspaper myself for the past five years, and have had at least one similar experience. Not long after I began work for the paper I overheard two distinguished playwrights chatting in the theater before curtain time:

"Will Kerr like this play? He's a Catholic, you know."

"Yes, but he's a very liberal Catholic. He used to work for *Commonweal*."

The Catholic who practices criticism outside the Catholic press is, in fact, suspect in both of the worlds he inhabits. The secular mind distrusts him because it fears that he will sooner or later abandon his pretense at criticism and reveal himself for the censor he is. And should he not begin to show the traits of a censor — should he not resort to the double standard characteristic of the Catholic press in general — he will as promptly be distrusted by Catholics. (He has succumbed to the secular spirit, they will say.) The unlucky fellow is often without honor in his home town and without honor abroad.

By and large, then, we have established a public arena in our time; the professional critic squares off in one corner, the professional censor in the other. Within American Catholicism, we have tended to assume that only one corner of the arena belongs to us. We have also done another thing; we have made of each individual work of art a smaller, separate arena, with art standing in one corner and morals in the other. The domain of art is entered belligerently.

3

IT WOULD BE pleasant if we could enjoy art more and fight about it less. It would be helpful to the production of art, I think, if we could somehow or other reduce the hostility that flares into active contention whenever criticism feels itself in danger of being circumscribed or whenever censorship feels itself in danger of being outlawed. An atmosphere of cheerful agreement about the purposes and effects of art might make us all more comfortable as we go to art; we should be able to leave our armor at home and go in a spirit of cheerful surrender to the delights the poet has contrived for us.

It seems doubtful to me, though, that we are going to bring about this state of beautiful rapport by pursuing our present programs. If rapport is sought at all nowadays, it is sought by dictation: the critic would like to unify society on the issue by making it impossible for any member of society to act as a censor; the opposition would like to achieve the same unity by turning every man into his own censor. Each hopes for an enforced harmony by demanding total allegiance to a single point of view. Unconditional surrender is what is wanted.

I'm not sure that any contest is ever settled by the outright elimination of one of the contestants. This is a recurring dream, like the Hatfields' dream that they are eventually going to kill *all* the McCoys. The McCoys are unpredictably fecund; there is always another baby hidden somewhere in the bushes. The notion that the world can be made safe for an enlightened point of view by carefully erasing from its face every other point of view, is, I suspect, an unrealistic one. Simple solutions invariably turn out to be too simple.

Let's look at the critical position first. Criticism has a simple solution: no censorship of any kind, ever. The root difficulty with this absolute position is that no one who holds it is able to hold it absolutely.

We are, in fact, constantly being confronted with instances in which men who are more or less on record as being opposed to all forms of censorship behave nevertheless like censors.

Critic Bosley Crowther's opposition to the principle of censorship is vigorous, consistent, clearly spelled out. Yet when, during World War II, Alfred Hitchcock made a motion picture called "Lifeboat," Mr. Crowther was seriously alarmed. The film showed a Nazi soldier outwitting (until the very end of the story) a whole boatload of Allies, and this at a time when our energies were engaged in a death struggle with the German soldiery. Mr. Crowther thought the film potentially harmful to our war effort, and asked for its withdrawal. I am sure that this particular critic would never have wished to suppress the film by legal means; but he was not above hoping that the producers could be persuaded to take it off the market. The film, as it happened, was not withdrawn; if it had been withdrawn at the critic's suggestion, both its producer and Mr. Crowther would have been entangled in a form of censorship.

Since World War II nearly everyone directly

17

connected with the entertainment arts has been involved in a running question of censorship; what plays and films shall be sent abroad to represent us, and what plays and films had best — if possible — be kept at home? Behind the discussions lurk very real fears: the Russians may make use of our own films to discredit us; other nations may, as an aftermath of the war, hold certain misconceptions about us and certain highly developed prejudices against us that might be further fed by a careless circulation of American plays. The right of government authorities, sponsoring theatrical tours, to make a cautious selection of materials has not really been questioned. Beyond this, various members of the theatrical professions have been willing to serve on advisory committees devoted to the same end: the winnowing out of "representative" and "unrepresentative" entertainments for foreign exhibition. At the meetings of such committees the word "censorship" is never heard; there is simply an honest and earnest effort made to send "the best" abroad. Yet "the best" does not under all circumstances mean "the best aesthetically"; it may mean "the best to represent us," especially when there seems to be a clash between aesthetic and representative values. A double standard is apt to crop up; the ultimate weight does not always lie with art. Though the decisions of such groups — and of the government itself — are sometimes subjected to mild debate in the letter columns of the press, there is no real formal opposition — certainly no suggestion of legal opposition — to the general practice of considered selection, no fierce insistence that our officials support every sort of art work without fear or favor. In general, no violation of artistic freedom is thought to be involved; to the degree that it might be involved, it is thought to be merely sensible.

On a recent trip to England I was startled by the intensity with which a number of Americans stationed in London condemned the release there of the film "From Here to Eternity." The people I talked to were sophisticates; they would, I think, have swiftly rejected the charge that they were in any way pro-censorship. No one of them specified any machinery for withholding the film; it wasn't clear whether they favored a government ban on English distribution or a silent self-sacrifice on the part of its producers. They were sure of only one thing: that the film had severely embarrassed them in their working relationship with the English, that it had acted to confirm an already widespread feeling that the American army was a brutal and brutalizing force. "The film ought not to have been shown here" became a familiar, vaguely resentful phrase.

Some years ago, when a disillusioned and somewhat sentimentalized pacifism was very much the order of the day, Irwin Shaw wrote a bitter anti-war play called "Bury the Dead." The play was almost cruel in its opposition to cruelty; certainly it left no room for the notion of a possibly just, necessary, or morally profitable war. The work was given wide international circulation. As World War II descended upon us, Mr. Shaw suddenly withdrew the production rights of the play; presumably he did not wish it to be used to discredit American participation in the battle against fascism. I doubt that Mr. Shaw would ever have gone on record as favoring censorship any more than he would have gone on record as favoring war; yet in this instance he acted as his own censor. I do not remember hearing his act criticized, in any quarter; in general, I think, the removal of the play from circulation was regarded as a patriotic, thoroughly honorable move.

The current outcry against certain types of "comic books" is so familiar to us all that it needs no documentation here. It might be pointed out, however, that opposition to the "violence," "sex," and "sadism" found in some of our drugstore juvenilia does not come exclusively, or even principally, from those religious sources normally identified with censorship. The most elaborate and emphatic denunciations have been written by lay psychiatrists for secular publications primarily devoted to literary criticism of the "purest" sort; or they have come from the sophisticated liberal strongholds inhabited by men like Walter Lippmann.

Most of us remember hearing something about a British-made film version of "Oliver Twist," with Alec Guiness in the role of Fagin. If our memories are vague, it is because very few of us managed to see the film. Upon its release in New York City there was considerable alarm over the patent Jewishness of the arch-scoundrel Fagin. No one suggested that Mr. Guiness had played the part badly, or even prejudicially. No one suggested that its producer had intended an anti-Semitic thrust. But there was fear in the air: fear that a perfectly well-executed and perfectly well-intentioned work of art might inadvertently feed the venom of such anti-Semites as already existed. It might add an ounce of fuel to a fire that is always ready to break out. The very fact that it contained one notoriously vicious character who was also a Jew was enough to make it — like "The Merchant of Venice," which has lately been suppressed in several American communities — a doubtful work for mass circulation.

"Oliver Twist" was not made the object of a legal attack. It is possible that Jewish pressure groups, acting wholly within their rights in a democratic society, helped to curtail its showings. It is possible that the producer of the film came to share the fear that the role of Fagin might be widely misinterpreted. It is possible that the theater chains, nervous as always about the effect of controversy upon the box office, simply decided not to book the picture. In any case, it was not widely booked; in effect, it disappeared from the screens of America. Though the portrait of Fagin, and the right of the artist to make such a portrait, was defended in the letter columns of the press during the original New York showing, I cannot recall any later demand of any intensity that the film be more generally distributed. A kind of silent, and apparently unregretted, censorship was effectively practiced.

Thus, on all sides and in an interesting variety of ways, the secular world is engaged in a practical — if not a formal — exercise of censorship. Men who would not for a moment tolerate the thought of official proscription are themselves active in forms of unofficial proscription. The instinct, it would seem, rises in every man.

I do not think we can question the sincerity of the man who is on record as being opposed to the principle of censorship and who yet urges the withdrawal of "Lifeboat," the man who worries about the effect of certain American plays on postwar Europe, or the man who is silent about "Oliver Twist."

In a good many cases, it never occurs to the critic, writer, or secular onlooker that he is engaged in censorship at all. Censorship, by and large, is identified with religious and moral taboos. The word instantly brings to mind a series of associations involving sexual frankness, physical display, or the kind of irreverence that Rosselini's "The Miracle" was in some quarters thought to foster. Mention "censorship" to the most sophisticated student of the arts and he will — despite the fact that the term turns up daily in dispatches from Washington — assume that you are talking about something related to sensuality.

Because censorship is so indelibly equated with moral alarms, its actual practice in other areas — political, social, diplomatic — simply does not seem to be censorship. Actually, any sort of act — whether it is overtly or discreetly accomplished — that involves the temporary suppression of certain materials toward what is thought to be the common good is an act of censorship.

All such acts will be intended, by their sponsors, as protective acts designed to safeguard or foster the general health of the community. The secular world today is primarily concerned with the political and social health of its members; it will tend, when it acts censorially, to act within these areas. Religion, on the other hand, is principally concerned with the moral and theological health of its specific communities and of the community at large; when *it* acts censorially, it will focus upon these ends.

Each of these two forces — or governments, if you wish — is saying the same thing: at this particular moment in time there is a higher good to be served than the good of art. (To take an absolute anti-censorial position it is necessary to take the position that there is no good, at any time or under any circumstances, higher than the good of art.) For the Church, the salvation of individual souls is a higher good than the good of art. For Walter Lippmann, the mental health of children is to be preferred to the uncontrolled dissemination of comic-book "art." For some Americans in England, the reputation of the United States and the United States Army bulks as a larger matter than the right to show a particular film. For Bosley Crowther, the political energy of our forces in wartime is momentarily more important than the freedom of an artist to exhibit his wares. Pressing needs tend to shift values around; there are times, it seems, when men wholeheartedly devoted to the cause of art reluctantly assign to the values of art a secondary place.

I think we must face the fact that all men, sooner or later, do behave in this way. The censorial principle leaps to life whenever the common good is thought to be threatened; a man may hold art dear but, when it seems necessary to make a choice between art and something he holds dearer, he will nerve himself to the unpleasant decision. One may argue that the choice is never truly necessary, that the conflict of interests is only an apparent, never a real, one. A difficulty remains: at the time of decision, in the face of alarm, there is insufficient elbowroom for a patient, careful disentangling of rival claims. Philosophers have not done it, in a general way, over something more than two thousand years; it would be extraordinary if an individual could do it, in a most particular way, at the moment when his child is exposed or his country menaced. What we are confronted with is a repeated, apparently universal response to supposed danger; whenever art is thought to give aid to the enemy — intentionally or unintentionally — there is a spontaneous urge to limit its circulation, to censor it.

My own experience is that every man and his brother winds up engaging in one or another kind of censorship. He does not, furthermore, limit his activities to protecting the immature; he is interested in protecting the presumably mature, too. And the secular world is every bit as much engaged in the practice as the religious. Under these circumstances — and simply acknowledging the way men *do* behave — it seems to me that the effort to abolish the principle of censorship is an unrealistic one, doomed to ultimate defeat. The all-out energies devoted to absolute abolition are likely to be wasted energies.

As a solution to our recurring problem, the

notion of outlawing any and every recourse to censorship is simply too sweeping, too much at variance with actual, and defensible, human habit. In a sense, it is not a solution at all, not even for the man who considers himself committed to it; this man probably does not really want to make it impossible for the United States Government to keep obvious pornography out of the mails; he probably does not want to prevent that same government from exercising a certain selectiveness about what it sends abroad. What he really wants to do is limit the exercise of censorship — limit it severely, perhaps, but still only limit it. Unfortunately, the extravagance of his stand prevents him from even trying to define such limitations as he might wish to impose. He has given himself a strong battle cry, but a weak tactical position.

4

IN ORDER TO swing around and look at the ambiguities that haunt the censorial, rather than the critical, point of view, suppose we begin by acknowledging the validity of the censorial principle. Let's say — if only for the purpose of argument — that the human instinct toward censorship is not only a recurring one but also a defensible one. Let's say that man is within his rights in holding that, under certain painful conditions, some other and "higher" good may take precedence over the good of art.

Even when the censor has been granted his power to function, the act he performs remains an extraordinary one — an act having, even when it is most perfectly conceived and most perfectly executed, extraordinary limitations inherent in its nature.

It is, to begin with, a *political* act, something done as part of the governing process; it is not, and never can be, a critical act taking serious account of the creative or aesthetic processes.

Yet each political act performed in this area is performed upon something that is not in its nature political. When a government makes a decision, say, about the need for additional taxes, it is acting upon matter that is wholly within its competence. A political judgment is made about a political matter; taxation is conceived as a legitimate function of government, government is conceived — in part — as an agency capable of taxing. There is complete harmony between the thing being treated and the treatment that is being given it; there are no loose ends left dangling. The decision made may be wise or unwise; but it cannot be functionally inappropriate. The tool and the hand wielding the tool were made to fit.

All this is, of course, elementary. The moment, though, that a governor is asked to use his political equipment and his political power on a structure that is essentially nonpolitical, a terrible ambiguity arises. Art does have criteria that are other than political (a painting may be wonderfully patriotic and utterly worthless, a play may be morally spotless and aesthetically absurd). Art has, in fact, no ready political criteria at all, and the governor asked to deal with it is asked to deal with something that is, in one very important sense, outside his competence.

The question he asks himself is this: am I, as a responsible governor, obligated to act against this work in order to protect my charges from possible danger? (This is a political question.) He does not ask: what is the artistic merit of this work — is it beautiful, is it well written, is it perfectly proportioned? (These are aesthetic questions.) In short, though the object at hand is an object which can be validly measured only by aesthetic criteria, the only valid questions the governor can ask are political questions.

He is limited to these questions for several reasons. In the first place, he is simply not qualified to ask any others. He is not, by training or equipment, an art critic. To act as though he were would be to expose himself to quick and thoroughly justified ridicule. (Being President of the United States does not, as we have lately seen, necessarily improve a man's taste in music; nor does sound musical taste automatically equip a man to become President of the United States.) And to ask that, in future, all men placed in positions of political authority bring with them sufficient training in aesthetics to handle the occasional "art" crises that come up is to ask the impossible; the problem is not going to be solved by a foolish idealism.

Furthermore, even if such a paragon — a sound critic and a sound censor in the same body — were to turn up, his verdicts would, to the degree that they were aesthetically arrived at, be extra-legal and arbitrary. There is no such thing as a political power to say what is, and what is not, art. Art is not art by fiat. A man may be given the authority to make political decisions about art; he cannot be given the authority to make aesthetic decisions about art that are legally binding. Not that this last hasn't been tried; the French Academy once had a fling at it, and the Russians are doing it now. The theoretical absurdity of the effort becomes plain the moment it is reduced to practice. The censor, even when he has been duly authorized to perform his particular task, has neither the equipment nor the authorization to introduce aesthetic considerations into that performance. He is limited to making a frankly one-sided decision about an admittedly two-sided matter.

In fact, a censor will be a good censor — politically speaking — in proportion as he maintains a strict indifference to aesthetic values. A man may, for instance, be in charge of a classroom filled with sixteen-year-old boys. He may be called upon to decide whether or not to circulate, by way of art study, a series of nudes. Experienced art critics may tell him that these are very good nudes; they may in fact be very good nudes. His decision, however, might be irrelevantly, even improperly influenced by consideration of their quality. In his position he cannot really ask, "Since these are excellent nudes, oughtn't they be circulated as widely as possible?" He must ask himself, "Do my charges have, at this stage of their development, the maturity, the emotional stability, the objectivity to look at nudes and value them for what they are?" This second question bypasses the whole matter of artistic merit, is phrased without reference to it; the nudes might be good or bad without altering its essential inquiry. If the man's primary responsibility is the mental and moral stability of those under his supervision, the issue of merit does not come up in any important way. Introducing it might cut across the psychological reality of the situation at hand and compromise the man in the discharge of his legitimate duties.

Similarly — to revert to an example we've already used — the official who has been asked to make a policy decision about the best American materials to send abroad will arrive at a realistic judgment by suppressing the issue of aesthetic superiority. Let's say that his final choice rests between two plays: one of greater aesthetic merit containing a built-in criticism of American life that might be made into an unfortunate symbol abroad, and one of lesser aesthetic merit — it is assumed that all of the plays brought before him have *some* merit or they would not be up for consideration — but without the sort of incidental content that would be vulnerable to propagandistic abuse. The official will exercise his function properly by resisting the aesthetic charms of the first and nominating the more "representative" second for export; that is what his office has been created for, it is what he has been assigned to do.

Thus it was no surprise this morning — September 28, 1955 — to pick up the New York *Times* and run across a familiar construction in connection with the proposed (and rejected) government financing of a Russian tour of "Porgy and Bess":

"State Department officials explained today that cost and political considerations had combined to bring about the decision, even though they recognized the folk opera as one of the most effective cultural representations the United States could send abroad. . . . They said they felt that such a tour was 'politically premature.' "

Here even the "representative" values of the work are acknowledged — and then dismissed in favor of a political strategy indifferent to art.

Again, the forces that led to the silent, and apparently voluntary, retirement of "Oliver Twist" were obliged — if their mission was to be successful — to ignore any claim the film may have had to quality. The matter of intention was dismissed; the producers' intentions may have been wholly honorable. The matter of aesthetic value was dismissed; everything in the picture may have been superbly wrought. Even the matter of possible anti-Semitic content was dismissed; the film may have contained no anti-Semitic material at all but may merely have been accidentally subject to anti-Semitic "use" by professional bigots. All concerns other than the directly political — the possible effect of the film upon the orderly conduct of society — were ruled irrelevant. The actual censoring of the film became an exclusively political act, and the almost universal silence that followed the act suggested that most intelligent men had approved the political process.

The process remains, however, a left-handed one. It disposes of a work of art without reference to the standards that make it art. It judges a thing not according to its own nature, but according to the nature of something outside it — the behavior of men, the state of the world, the sound of the wind. The thing judged and the judgment made have no interior harmony, no functional appropriateness to one another. The relation between the office of censor and the living actuality of the object censored is, humanly speaking, an imperfect one.

Even when the principle of censorship is admitted as valid, this disproportion between method and matter remains an alarming limitation upon its possibly judicious exercise. Because the censor does not and cannot evaluate the whole object that confronts him, the chances of his being wrong — and of thereby doing damage to the interests of art — are serious.

5

THERE IS A second disturbing difficulty that must always accompany any exercise of the principle. The censorial act is, in its nature, a *prudential* act.

Prudence is a virtue. At its best, as the dictionary tells us, it is the "ability to regulate and discipline oneself through the exercise of the reason." But the dictionary goes on to remark that the term "implies caution, circumspection, or economy, especially in practical affairs." That is to say, the reason is exercised not upon a body of known facts, available certainties; it is exercised with forethought, upon materials which have not yet taken conclusive shape. Prudence is anticipatory; it looks forward to what *may* happen.

As we habitually use the term, "prudence" does not pretend to act in areas of certainty. The censor, behaving prudently, does not say to himself — or to anyone else — "I *know* this work of art will be harmful to all men, or even to some men." (Obviously, he doesn't know; he has no carefully tabulated results before him as he makes his anticipatory judgment.)

The censor simply says, "I *think* this work will prove harmful," or "This work *might* prove harmful," or "The *possible* danger attaching to this work is great enough to require my acting prudently."

Prudence is a virtue to be exercised where a degree of ignorance exists. We do not think of it, or speak of it, as though it had any other character.

We do not, for instance, suggest to a man that he be prudent about stepping off the top of the Empire State Building. No one is ever heard to announce that it would be prudent not to cut one's throat.

Prudence is not invoked in these situations because there is a fairish certainty about the outcome. In either of them I can act *wisely* — out of a clear and complete knowledge — or I can act insanely, flying in the face of my knowledge. But I cannot cut my throat circumspectly, or step off that ledge cautiously and on the alert for some subsequent danger. There is room for reasonable or unreasonable behavior, but there is no room at all for prudence.

Where the outcome is known, where there are available facts to be reckoned with, wisdom is called for. Where the outcome is uncertain, where there are as yet no clear facts but only reasonable apprehensions, prudence is called for.

I act prudently whenever there is possible but not conclusive danger, and I do it to avoid a danger that is not wholly upon me. I want to put myself — or the persons I am charged with supervising — out of the path of a threat that may or may not materialize. When I act prudently, I am always trying to keep *ahead* of the storm.

But in this precautionary behavior there is, once more, a limitation upon the perfection of the censorial act. The censor is not acting out of clear knowledge. He is acting in a *kind* of ignorance.

There is no way around this theoretical — and sometimes very practical — natural imperfection in the act. The censor is, by the nature of his duties, bound to act before the crucial event has taken place, before the harm that might be done is actually done, before there is any factual information at hand to confirm the danger he fears. The censor who waits until the world has been overturned — if this is a possible effect of art — is obviously a very poor censor. The responsible man is expected to avert the presumed catastrophe; and if it never takes place as a result of his forethought there is never going to be any conclusive evidence that his action was necessary. He has got to take a *chance* on being right, whatever history may think of him later.

Obviously, the risk of error would be greatly reduced if the censor had at his disposal a set of facts and figures referring to other, earlier cases. Since he must keep a jump ahead of the facts in the case at hand, it would help him a great deal if he could consult genuine evidence on the ill effects of art in a thousand prior instances, or on the ill effects of art *generally*.

Unhappily, he has none that any scientist would consider conclusive. A priest who has sat in the confessional might tell him that certain harmful effects of certain works of art on individual personalities have been reported to him; but he cannot offer any acceptable formal tabulation of these effects. A man who has worked in London might tell him that, in his own immediate experience, a certain film has done a certain degree of harm abroad; but this is only a factually unsubstantiated opinion. A long tradition out of the past, gathering force by its very age, might suggest to him that since men of every known time and every known culture have assumed the possible ill effects of art, he might honorably assume them, too. He is still buttressing his position with an assumption.

The most thorough attempt I know of to get behind the individual experience, the generalized opinion, and the traditional assumption is Mortimer Adler's investigation of the "effect" problem in his 1937 work *Art and Prudence*. The work, though it has not really been superseded, is neglected now. One reason for the neglect, I suspect, is that it offers us no comfort. Mr. Adler, if I read him rightly, closes his examination of all the sociological studies available to him with the submission that we have not yet successfully measured the effects of art. He does not presume to say that art has no effects, good or bad; he says that, even where effects are indicated, the precise character of these effects is not known. (It may be shown that a child who has been to an exciting movie tosses more frequently in his sleep on that night than on another; it is not yet certain whether the increased tossing makes for better, or worse, sleep.) We cannot tell ourselves that we are in possession of scientifically demonstrable facts in this matter — not even in past cases that might be turned into guideposts. We act now, when we act censorially, on matter that has not yet given us firm evidence of its harmfulness. And we act on the basis of prior assumptions that have not been turned, by accurate measurements, into certainties.

Indeed, when we do decide to act prudently, we do it precisely because we are hampered by ignorance. The sword is double-edged. Being ignorant, we are obliged to act prudently. Being prudent, we are in constant danger of making decisions — decisions that may curtail the operation of something intrinsically good — on the basis of insufficient evidence.

The principle of censorship may be accepted as valid. Acts of censorship are exceedingly difficult to perfect.

6

AT ITS MOST valid, then, every act of censorship labors under at least two unhappy limitations. Being a political act, it refuses to treat a work of art *as* a work of art, fails to take full account — in passing judgment — of the nature of the thing judged. As a prudential act, it operates within an area of relative ignorance rather than within an area of demonstrable knowledge.

If we are to accept the principle of censorship as valid, we are simultaneously bound to take note of the inadequacies, ambiguities, and uncertainties that must attach to its practical exercise. That is to say, any positive act of censorship ought to be regarded as an extraordinary act to be performed only under the most extraordinary circumstances.

I'd say that there were certain minimum conditions for the just performance of so extraordinary an act:

It ought to be undertaken only by authorities so responsibly placed that to fail to take action would be to fail to discharge a clear and specific duty to the governed. (It ought never to be the province of amateurs, or of the politically unaccredited.)

It ought to be performed only after profound deliberation, after the most painstaking examination of conscience on the part of the censor. (Since even the most profound deliberation cannot lead the censor to scientific certainty, the snap judgment ought to be regarded as an open invitation to error.)

It ought to be performed, when the act is finally thought necessary, with the utmost reluctance, with transparent regret. (This need not be a matter of crocodile tears; let's just say that the act ought never to be performed *enthusiastically*.)

And every act of censorship should, after the fact, be subjected to the most careful, continuing scrutiny, to constant and hopeful re-examination, to revision the moment revision seems politic. (The books should never be regarded as closed; no act of censorship should ever be thought a triumph.)

If we are going to submit to the practical need for a censor, we had best have a clear picture of him: as a man who has been given an unattractive and unrewarding job to do, who does it only because the specific responsibility has been thrust upon him, who knows that his political responsibility may be at odds with the interests of art, who is prepared to override the interests of art only in the most extreme urgencies, who goes about his business with little confidence in his own rectitude and after an anguished examination of his own motives, who comes to his rare proscriptions in genuine pain, and who thereafter hopefully and steadily reviews his work toward possible revision. The good censor would be, I think, something close to a tragic hero. He would not, if he had any awareness of the complexities with which he was dealing, ever be a happy zealot.

The authorized censor is required to be prudent. He is also required, considering the imperfection of his tools and the comparative ignorance in which he must use them, to be *prudently* prudent.

7

DOES CENSORSHIP, as we generally encounter it in America today, behave more or less in the manner of our responsible, sensitive, reluctant, tormented ideal image? I'm afraid it does not.

Like that critical mind that hopes to end the contest once and for all by legally destroying the principle of censorship and thus forcibly committing the whole of society to its point of view, the censorial mind aims at total victory by total involvement. It, too, is out for permanent victory, and the key to permanent victory is the capture of everyman for the cause. Everyman may come willingly; or he may be browbeaten into worrying about his livelihood. But if the enemy — the critical camp — is going to see to it that there can be no such thing as a censor, then the prudent feel that they must try very hard to make censors out of everybody.

In trying to capture the allegiance of the whole society for its point of view — and if not the allegiance then the obedience — censorship as a movement undertakes a series of programs. There is the propaganda program: the dissemination of the idea that art is something to be watched, and confined, at all times; whatever organs of the press are available — the Catholic diocesan press is an especially fertile field — are steadily supplied with cries of alarm.

There is the implicit encouragement of amateur censorship, the widespread suggestion that this is an activity in which all men should, in conscience, participate.

And there is, as a quite logical consequence of so much encouragement, the actual proliferation of censorial bodies throughout the society — beginning at the top with authorized bodies and spreading downward to include a horde of volunteer bodies having no authorization at all. Indeed, the distinction between the legitimate censor and the amateur censor becomes lost in the profusion.

Most seriously — and most successfully, from the enthusiastically censorial point of view — there is the firm establishment within the society, or within substantial segments of the society, of a censorial *attitude* toward art as the one essential and necessary attitude. That is to say, the average man is placed in a certain position in relation to art; he forms an habitual stance, a way of looking at and thinking about a visible object that is preconditioned, governed by a single emphasis, strongly and even prejudicially oriented toward just one of the many surfaces that art may be said to possess. By the time the man susceptible to censorial pressures has actually been subjected to the bombardment now possible, he is no longer capable of coming to art with an open mind, or an appreciative mind, or even a critical mind. He comes to it with a censorial mind — in a shocking number of instances with an *exclusively* censorial mind.

Once the practice of censorship has passed from the hands of the formally accredited into the hands of semiaccredited and unaccredited volunteers, it seems to take on the weight and the irresistibility of a glacier. We have all, as Americans and as Catholics, seen this movement at work.

As Americans, most of us have probably lived at one time or another in communities which forbade Sunday entertainments. (I know that, for most of my own youth, I had to cross the city line if I wanted to see a movie on a Sunday afternoon.) It should be remembered that this is a form of censorship — a specific limitation placed upon the circulation of art — and that it reflects the censorial state of mind in its clear implication that art is in some way not "holy," that its pursuit on a day of worship could only contaminate the day.

As Americans, most of us have probably lived in communities where motion pictures were subjected to review, and cutting, by local censors. Obviously, there is some legal accreditation involved here; it is, however, of that parasitical kind which begins in volunteer activity and eventually achieves official status so that the censor can be paid, which represents a vast diffusion of censorial authority rather than a careful concentration at a responsible and answerable center, which opens itself to almost certain error by making the office a political plum to be filled by a party hack or an influential matron of less than spectacular intelligence. (I am almost an authority on this matter. As a youngster I was very friendly with my home-town projectionist, who, after he had finished clipping a new film at the order of an elderly and rather pugnacious lady, used to give me the clips for my home library.)

As Catholics we continue to be surrounded by official proscription, by proscription that is official "but not binding," by additional advice from pulpit and press that is not necessarily official but is nonetheless impressive, and by amateur assistance from the youngest of school children. Indeed, as the glacier has begun to show signs of melting in American secular life, American Catholicism has seemed eager to rush new ice into the breach.

There is, theoretically, a clearer distinction between authorized and amateur practices in Catholic thought than in secular thought; the hierarchical Church has been careful to define the functions of its members. At the moment, however, such distinctions have in practice become seriously blurred; the movement toward capturing the mind of everyman for the censorial cause has been especially successful among Catholics. A power that is meant to be an extraordinary power has become the most casual, commonplace, and matter-of-fact of usages; it has infiltrated the daily thinking, and the daily conduct, of the average lay Catholic to the point where a free-association test might draw the word "censorship" as a natural response to the given word "art." In this spontaneous response I think there would be very few formal lines drawn.

Thus few contemporary Catholics would be able to tell you what is and what is not on the official Index of the Church; and some of those who *do* tell you are sadly ill informed. But nearly every lay Catholic can tell you what current films and plays are on the dozens of "little Indexes" that pursue them from the pages of diocesan newspapers, devotional magazines, magazines created especially for the purpose of giving moral ratings to "best sellers," and — finally — from the lips of his well-meaning Catholic neighbors. It is, as a matter of fact, exceptionally easy for him to tell you what is presently proscribed or marked as suspect because, sooner or later in the shower of admonitions, nearly everything is.

I know that this remark sounds facetious, if not downright irresponsible. It is uncomfortably close to the truth. A few seasons ago a New York playgoer who took his Catholic magazine listings to heart would have felt free to see exactly one legitimate entertainment during the entire season. That entertainment was "Howdy Mr. Ice of 1950."

Nor is it at all unusual to pick up a diocesan newspaper and discover, perhaps on its front page, an attack upon a local producing group for having the effrontery to present Oscar Wilde's "The Importance of Being Earnest." I sometimes think that if a dutiful Catholic correlated all the gratuitous advice that is given him on the subject of entertainment and conscientiously abided by it

45

he would have no choice but to spend his evenings in the nearest bar.

Some of the more extravagant examples of censorial advice may be dismissed as the routine, and not terribly representative, excesses which must crop up in the course of any worthwhile human activity. I do not think they can be so dismissed. They reflect, and further encourage, a state of mind that has become second nature to American Catholics: a state of mind that takes one question that may be asked about the arts and blows it up to such gross proportions that all other questions cease to exist.

The average American Catholic is by now so indoctrinated in the censorial attitude that, on approaching a work of art, he never does ask: is it a good work of art or a bad work of art, will I like it or will I be disappointed in it? The *first* question he asks — and often the *only* question he asks — is: is it a decent or an indecent work?

I had no idea how widespread, or how all-consuming, this attitude was until, some seven or eight years ago, I went on a short lecture tour of the Middle West. I had been leading a comparatively sheltered existence at the Catholic University of America and was quite unprepared for the rigors of what was apparently held to be the "official" Catholic position on art.

Before each of the scheduled lectures I was hospitably greeted by a committee, sometimes a family or two and sometimes a substantial gathering in a nearby hotel, for dinner and a bit of ice-breaking conversation. The conversation, I gradually discovered, was always to open in the same way: "What are we going to do about all these filthy Broadway plays?"

On at least eight successive evenings, in eight different communities, at eight convivial dinners, the same introductory phrase turned up. Nor was it a mere conventional opener to more ranging topics; on each occasion it remained the single and virtually inexhaustible subject. Again, it was not a subject to be debated, it was an agreed-upon condemnation to be repeated as often and as vehemently as possible. During the entire time I never ran across any variations in attitude. No one *ever* asked, "Is there anything good to see in New York?"

At first I was irritated by what seemed to me a hostile atmosphere. But the faces around these tables were smiling, eager, patently cordial faces. Gradually I realized what my hosts were doing. They were putting me at my ease. I was a Catholic and I was going to talk about the arts. They knew, from previous experience, what a Catholic who was going to talk about the arts was going to say about the arts. They wanted me to know, as quickly as possible, that they were with me, heart and soul. They were sending up signals that said: go ahead, we know what you're here

47

for, we do agree, and you don't have to pull any punches. They were making me comfortable; what I had felt as hostility was actually the most considerate hospitality. Since, apparently, no earlier lecturer had ever taken any other tack, they were doing the courteous, the expected, and the obviously necessary thing.

It was perfectly clear from the conversation, by the way, that they were familiar with the plays and films that most frequently came under attack; they *had* seen them, were able to discuss them in detail, had not — in general — permitted their fears to keep them away. (The authorized censor is obliged to worry about "other" people who are his charges; the unauthorized censor borrows this habit of mind and goes right on worrying about "other" people, while getting around himself a good bit.) But if their practical behavior toward art was still reasonably loose, their formal attitudes toward art were unshakably strict. Say "art" and you had said "danger."

I continue to be reminded of this eye-opening jaunt every time a pleasant young truck driver delivers beer to our house. This driver, a good Catholic, knows that I am in some way connected with the theater and, since he is an agreeable sort with a real flair for doing his work cheerfully, he will almost always toss in a word or two about my special interest. That is to say, he will mention a film he is staying away from because it is on "the list," or he will ask me whether a certain play is really all right to see, or he will, with an infectious grin and shake of the head, take his leave with the thought that, "Gee, they sure try to get away with it, don't they?"

A few years ago one of the neighbors' children was especially anxious about a speech she was to deliver before a school assembly devoted to Catholic Action, and, because my wife had at one time been a teacher of public speaking, she came to the house for help. Working upstairs, I could hear the words, formed in a seventh-grade classroom, that came piping out of this eleven-year-old. They advocated not only a constant vigilance toward all motion-picture entertainment, but an active picketing — by school children — of "lascivious" films. I remember wondering at the time if the girl knew what "lascivious" meant; I remember wondering, if she did know, whether she should have; and I wondered if, the next time I passed our local theater, I would be treated to the spectacle of a troop in blue jumpers carrying placards denouncing the sexual indiscretions of their elders.

At the present time we seem to begin indoctrinating the Catholic child in his attitude toward art in the earliest grades; he is taught, as soon as possible, to be suspicious. As he passes through high school — and becomes prey to the difficulties of adolescence — the emphasis on caution is doubled. As a maturing person, he is urged to stand in Church and pledge himself to renewed vigilance. As the head of a family, he is obviously obliged not only to be careful about his own contacts with art but to keep a watchful eye over his children's contacts.

The purpose of all this admonition is, of course, the formation of a "right" conscience, the ability to know a thing for what it is and to deal wisely with it. It is possible that the process does form a certain number of "right" consciences. It is fairly certain, I think, that it also forms something else: a habit of thinking of art as one of man's natural enemies, as a standing trap for the unwary, as a likely invitation to license, as a vehicle of beauty designed not simply to be beautiful but to lure man along the road to certain unlawful excesses, as something inherently and essentially corrupting rather than something inherently and essentially good. Art has been given its Puritan definition; it is a temptation.

With this training, it is not surprising that the average lay Catholic in America should, in his maturity, move toward the arts with a chip on his shoulder and a panicky apprehension in his breast. He is not conditioned to approach art with simple affection, candid enthusiasm, or any sort of confidence in its goodness. He is, rather, dressed in an armor that is not easily dented; he comes looking for the sly and sensual thrust that means to catch him off balance, for the calculated trick that the artist intends to play on him. He is morally nervous in the presence of anything attractive, more or less certain that attractiveness is in itself a fault — or perhaps a mask manufactured to conceal a fault. Art, for him, has an insidious root; he must sip at it warily for fear of being poisoned. The cup may be lifted to the lip, all right, but it must be lifted in a spirit of alert distrust.

The average American Catholic comes to art with the unfriendly eye and the suspicious sniff of a watchdog. He has been told, time and again, that his function *is* that of a watchdog; and if his bite is not always as bad as his bark, it is sharp enough to keep most purveyors of mass entertainment at a discreet and pacifying distance.

The mass has itself become the censor. The audience has, in effect, taken upon itself the extraordinarily difficult task of making and enforcing decisions of a political and prudential character. It has also, necessarily, diffused over a vast area the ambiguities and imperfections that attach to the censorial act.

8

WE HAVE SAID that the authorized censor must, because of the peculiar duty with which he is charged, be indifferent to the needs and nature of art. Turn the social mass into a hydra-headed censor and you are left with an entire society that is indifferent to the needs and nature of art.

What is an unfortunate but unavoidable limitation upon a legitimate practice becomes something like a smug and comfortable virtue in the righteous mass mind. If the official censor need not consider the specific claims of art in making his anguished decision, then *no one* need ever consider these claims — now that everyone is a censor. Since the average man has taken it upon himself to perform these precautionary duties, it is quite proper for the average man to dismiss any criteria for judging a work other than the political and prudential criteria we have mentioned. Thus the aesthetic criteria that the authorized censor has reluctantly put aside as irrelevant to his peculiar task are now lightly and even cheerfully put aside by the entire community. Art ceases to have laws of its own, even a character of its own. In the popular mind it becomes an appendage to morals, a possible "occasion of evil," a negation existing only in the sense that sin exists; it is very nearly viewed as a weakness in man that cannot be entirely overcome but that can be tempered to the point where it is relatively harmless.

Dealing with it, making decisions about it,

becomes easy. If a work is seen, after microscopic inspection, to contain nothing that could conceivably be considered a departure from the moral law, then it is a good work. There is nothing more to be said about it. If a work in some way seems to violate the moral law, to ignore the moral law, or even to explore the moral law too thoroughly — by this I mean that it examines the evil as well as the virtuous aspects of a moral conflict in some detail — then it is a dubious work. The only further thing to be done with a dubious work is to grade its dubiety, to determine whether or not our more adventurous adults may be able to indulge themselves without certain contamination.

Now I am not concerned here with the accuracy of the moral judgments offered. It is possible that every last one of them correctly evaluates the "risk" content of the work passing in review. (This isn't a likely state of affairs, considering the variety of hands now being put to the task; but let's say for the moment that the kind of evaluation attempted is in fact successfully made.) We are still confronted with the spectacle of an entire community reaching conclusions about art without having for a moment taken into consideration the qualities that make it art.

The result is — necessarily — a low level of taste in the community, perhaps the disappearance of taste altogether. The community no longer has any means at its disposal for distinguishing one piece of work from another provided both subscribe to the same moral code. A vulgar virgin is as good as a sensitively conceived virgin; the only thing that matters is that it is a virgin. A sentimental tale is as good as an honest tale so long as neither tale is offensive to the censorial rule-of-thumb. The values of honesty, accuracy, insight, sensitivity, proportion, and so on, disappear; they cease to be "values" because they play no part in the process of evaluation. In time, honesty cannot be distinguished from sentimentality, vulgarity from sensitivity. The tools have been dropped, awareness blunted, vision blurred. The community has become a community of bats operating on a sort of moral radar; it cannot see what it is carefully circling around.

The generally low taste of the Catholic community in America has been a minor scandal for quite a time now. It stares at us from the pages of the same diocesan newspapers that devote so much of their space to censorial exhortation; it stares at us — as we have long known — from our churches. Critical protests against all that is garish, saccharine, and simply badly executed have frequently been raised; if these have in general been ineffectual, it is because they have fallen upon indifferent ears — not upon stubborn ears, or ears that are passionately listening to some other siren song, but ears that have been trained not to hear anything at all that is spoken in the name of "art." Indifference is the rule – the censorial rule – diffused over a vast social structure.

It may be thought that a low level of taste is native to the mass, any mass, and that it is foolish to lament vulgarity in the workaday lives of the workaday crowd. The notion seems to me an evasive one, in itself a sample of indifferentism. Art at the folk level is often primitive, lacking in breadth, variety, and sophistication; but it is also capable, within its own circumscribed universe, of exquisite taste. Any man who really loves the thing he is working with quickly becomes adept at making qualitative distinctions regarding it; if anything, he tends to become a fanatic about quality, a contentious exponent of the "best." The instinct toward perfection is, I think, a natural one so long as there is some passion felt for the material at hand; taste follows enthusiasm, even when the object of a man's enthusiasm is only a cigar, a beer, or a ball team. To inhibit taste one must first kill love; after that, distinctions *won't* matter. I suspect, then, that the generally low level of Catholic taste is not something that has simply happened, a sample of natural sluggishness in the mass; it is more likely something that has been created, a kind of paralysis born of inculcated fear. Art may burn you; therefore keep your distance. At such a distance art becomes a gray blur in which no true colors can be identified. The mind that holds art in this discreet and wary relationship to it may be a "pure" mind; but it is also a mind that is insensitive and unresponsive to God-given values that are actually present.

If a low level of taste follows inevitably from the improperly diffused censorial practice of maintaining a sturdy indifference to aesthetic values, this low level is made a permanent condition by the improper diffusion of the second limitation inherent in the censorial act: the limitation that requires the censor to act in a kind of ignorance.

That is to say, the authorized censor *must* act before all the facts are in, *must* act without absolute knowledge. When everyman is turned into a censor, it follows that everyman is free to act in ignorance — out of impulse, habit, prejudice, or mere suspicion. Knowledge is thought to be generally unnecessary, perhaps even unbecoming. The urge to *know* the facts about art dries up; there is no longer any possibility of modifying or revising such habits of mind or levels of taste as now exist.

The assumption grows that knowledge of art — the kind of knowledge that would help us to make qualitative distinctions, or the kind of knowledge that Mortimer Adler was looking for in his study of the possible effects of art — could not really be of use to us in making the kind of decisions we are committed to. To pursue an aesthetic would be to move steadily away from the "decent-indecent" slide rule that has proved so convenient and so cheerfully complete. The road ahead of us has only two forks: the fork marked "prudence" leads to safety; the fork marked "knowledge" leads only to "art-for-art's-sakism." Best to close off the second road altogether; why risk any discoveries that might complicate and confuse the issue?

Naturally, the choice between these two courses is not stated so baldly by those who effectively insist upon its being made. No one in his right mind is going to come out against the pursuit of "knowledge." Yet the pressure against that pursuit in censorially minded circles is sufficiently strong to attach an unholy aura to the word "aesthetic" and to limit the positions a man may take to just two. Only yesterday a young priest who is working on a doctoral dissertation in the field stopped by to ask a few questions about my reviewing work. When I expressed the opinion that a daily reviewer ought to try to make aesthetic rather than censorial evaluations, he looked up quickly and said "Oh, you're for art-for-art's-sake?" There were no other possibilities: one was either a censor and functioned as a censor, or one was automatically committed to a single, seedy, very specific and largely discredited philosophy of the late nineteenth century. "Aesthetic" and "art-for-art's-sake" are synonymous terms;

"art-for-art's-sake" is an obvious dead end; therefore "aesthetics" is an obvious dead end. The door to any sort of aesthetic "knowledge" is promptly closed. Though the young man had faithfully read his way through Mortimer Adler, Jacques Maritain, and Leonard Callahan, and though he was studying under a distinguished moral theologian, no conceivable alternative had presented itself to him. He inhabits a climate.

This climate is best symbolized for me by a memory. When I was extremely young, I succeeded in writing and directing a musical comedy for my local parish. The pastor, a good and generous man, wanted to pay me a compliment. He did so by comparing some doggerel I had written by way of lyrics to the work of Shakespeare. Favorably, that is to say. I was not so young that I wasn't at least mildly embarrassed, and I rather heatedly launched into an explanation of why Shakespeare might be thought my superior. The pastor listened considerately, smiled, shrugged his shoulders, and at last murmured, "*Cui bono?*"

The Catholic community in this country, then, exhibits not only a relatively low level of taste but a confidence that that taste need not be improved. The effort to improve it is most often met with either an open hostility (the quick cry of "art-sakist") or a philosophical shrug (*"Cui bono?"*). Fear has cut off that natural affection which might have produced natural taste; indifference has cut off that serious study which might have produced knowledge. The subject of art, in all of its aspects, is conveniently kept at arm's length.

The paralysis of taste and the resistance to knowledge which follow from any vast diffusion of censorial attitudes are by no means confined to the Catholic community. One has only to pick up a daily newspaper to run across random samples of the process at work. Without going out of my way to look for evidence, I can turn over the page of the New York *Times* at breakfast and come across, say, the information that the Joint Legislative Committee on Problems of the Aging has just issued a 160-page report — compiled by four Senators and four New York Assemblymen — accusing Hollywood of discriminating against the elderly.

"The Hollywood approach to the life-cycle calls for a heroine of about 23, with a hero 25 to 30, while the villain's role must be played by a 40-plus actor," says the report. It would, by the way, be fascinating to see the evidence for this, if any exists. But I don't imagine we need go into the matter of whether or not the statement is true, or, if it *is* true whether or not there mayn't be good reasons for its being true. This is the censorial mind at work in the secular community, attending the movies with an intellectual habit that is alert, "corrective," and gloriously obtuse.

It would be no trick to multiply examples.

The habit of mind is, however, to be found at its most intense in the parochial Catholic atmosphere. Let's say we are attending a performance of the play "Ladies in Retirement" — as I once did — in a Catholic girls' college. "Ladies in Retirement" is a murder melodrama, and at one point in its action the villainess of the piece is seen to steam open an envelope in order to read a purloined letter. One of the good nuns teaching in the college was seriously alarmed that the play should have been performed at all; it would, she insisted, instruct the students in the niceties of this immoral practice. Visions of six hundred girls steaming open each other's letters came swiftly to this prudent mind.

It isn't easy to take this sort of complaint seriously. Yet it has quite serious implications; a faculty member of a liberal-arts college has never asked or attempted to answer the question, "What *are* the liberal arts?" It is clear that no effort has been made to answer the specific questions: (*a*) what is a play? (*b*) what is the relationship of one episode in a play to the play as a whole? (*c*) to what degree does an audience ever imitate a play?

A college might be thought the very place to ask and answer such questions. The censorial response has, however, become so fixed by long training that it cannot now be dislodged. Even in an environment committed to intellectual inquiry, the one habitual question takes precedence over all others: does the play give bad example? The mind is conditioned to look for infringements of the moral code; looking for them, it is bound to find them; not knowing how to relate them to an aesthetic structure it is bound to condemn them.

It should be plain, I think, that no work of art could hope to pass this kind of scrutiny. That is one reason why, in the present atmosphere, very few works of art do; Shakespeare must be a long time dead before his obvious bad example can be charitably overlooked.

The instance of "Ladies in Retirement" may sound silly, so silly that we feel perfectly free to dismiss it as exceptional. But so long as we fail to ask the essential questions, it is not necessarily any sillier or more exceptional than a hundred other judgments we make. So long as we work willingly in ignorance, and shy away from the very effort at knowledge, how can we be sure which of our judgments *is* silly?

9

LIKE THE CRITICAL position that would deny society the right to appoint any man a censor, the rival position that appoints every man a censor represents an unworkable extreme. Each position attempts to win the day for its own point of view by denying the validity of any other point of view. Because the world is not quite so simple as this, because there are two rival claims — the claim of art and the claim of the community — that need to be brought into sensitive balance, the man who insists on a sweeping solution quickly finds himself in difficulties. The critic, in theory, places the good of art above the good of the community; and then finds himself making nervous little noises about the effect of "Lifeboat" or "Oliver Twist" or comic books upon the community. The censor places the good of the community above the good of art; and then finds himself, if he has not divested himself of all sensitivity, embarrassed to death by the shabby art he has helped produce.

The battle is, really, a battle of fears — the critic fears that the moralist is going to degrade art, the moralist fears that the critic is going to seduce souls — and acute fear always does tend to produce hysterical responses. To pursue the battle upon its present terms is, I think, to pursue it hysterically — and probably to fail to resolve it.

Can it be resolved? Not quickly: of that we can be certain. And it is very probable that there is going to be some contention between the politician and the poet right down to the end of time, if only because these two work with such different tools and therefore distrust one another's methods. Art may remain a permanent football, and still survive; it has an odd habit of making some of its most graceful arabesques precisely when it is being kicked.

But are we entitled to rest on the assumption that harmony can never be had, that no agreement on the matter is possible? Such an assumption implies that knowledge itself is out of bounds for poor mankind, that no definition of the nature and influence of art can ever be achieved with sufficient clarity and sufficient persuasiveness to compel the mutual assent of our two contenders. Is it permissible for us — whether we are on the critical or the censorial side of the argument — to despair of definition, to dismiss the pursuit of genuine knowledge because genuine knowledge is so difficult to come by, to entrench ourselves firmly in our present boldly held opinions, and to battle it out in confident ignorance?

At the present time neither faction in the quarrel can be said to *know* — demonstrably, persuasively — the nature of the thing it is dealing with. In the heat of battle, any weapon that is momentarily effective seems to suffice. Criticism, for instance, has won most of its recent victories by equating art with journalism; it has, in certain successful court tests, freed the artist from censorial attack by lumping his activity with such other activities as now have a Constitutional guarantee of "freedom of speech." But is art essentially a vehicle of information? Is it essentially a vehicle of opinion? Or does it, in its uniqueness, need to be defended in some other way? (If, for instance, art should not be essentially a vehicle of information or essentially a vehicle of opinion, then victories such as these can easily be overthrown by the merest change in the emotional climate; nothing permanent has been won for art because nothing definitive has been said about art.)

If criticism has been willing to ascribe to art any character that will help bring about criticism's immediate objective, censorship has behaved in even more cavalier fashion; it has side-stepped the whole problem of definition and simply taken an effective swipe at the artist's and the distributor's pocketbook. Both sides are interested in devices that will work; whether the devices bring us any closer to an understanding of the battle we are fighting — an understanding so profound that it can be made to stick — is beside the question. So long as we get what we want we do not much care whether or not we have come by it legitimately.

There is, of course, a science of aesthetics; it belongs among the philosophical disciplines. No one engaged in the current struggle seems to feel that the tools of this discipline might be usefully applied to the problem before us. Certainly the tools have been little displayed during the controversy (I doubt that many among the comparatively few men familiar with them would accept the identification of art with editorial opinion that is assumed in the "freedom of speech" guarantee). Censorship will not even look at the tools; criticism — which should be much better acquainted with them — does not appear to think them relevant. When art is attacked, it is attacked on political grounds; when art is defended, it is defended on political grounds. Aesthetic grounds do not seem to exist.

Nor is anyone trying very hard to make them exist, to pull them forward out of the library of speculative thought into the contemporary arena. Though the Catholic tradition has been fed by the minds of such men as Augustine, Aquinas, and Newman — and is currently being enriched by Maritain — awareness of the aesthetic thread in this tradition is virtually nonexistent in those very circles most earnestly devoted to passing judgments on "art." In the mass mind there is, needless to say, no reflection at all of St. Thomas' enthusiasm for art as a human *necessity*. At the intellectual level — say, in the graduate schools of our universities — there is passing and fragmentary reference to these masters just as there is occasional course work in one or another phase of "art" or "aesthetics" (you will be lucky if the lone course in an institution isn't called "Moral Principles of Art and Drama"). But there is no true body of work to be undertaken, no room for the pursuit of a discipline beyond a fairly primitive historical survey, no recognition of aesthetics as a science in need of continuing and possibly profitable development, no intense conviction that knowledge might be had for the asking (and the labor) or that such knowledge might be directly applied to crises that are actually at hand. When, not long ago, a young man who had already — and hungrily — snatched at the smattering of aesthetic investigation offered him by two of our major Catholic universities dropped by to ask if I could direct him to any further course work, I could think of nowhere to send him. Such work as is being done at the moment amounts to a kind of underground, and a soon-bottled-up underground at that; a promising man may do a dissertation in the field while he is still a student, discover — shortly thereafter — that there is no demand for him as a teacher or scholar so long as he confines himself to his true interest, and — inevitably — drift off into other areas of study. The average student is not introduced to aesthetics; the aesthetically-minded student is stopped in his tracks.

I do not find the situation any better in our secular schools. While working on this lecture I was invited to speak at one of the three best-known American universities. I spent some time before the meeting chatting with a professor of

English who conducted most of the courses in drama. I asked him, in passing, whether or not a student doing historical surveys in drama could pick up a course — any kind of a course — in general aesthetics. He said yes: there was a single course in the philosophy department devoted to the subject; the student could take it in connection with his regular work. He was of the opinion, however, that the student would not derive any more useful information from it than he would from the professor's own one-semester course in Modern Drama. I haven't much doubt that the professor was right.

We aren't — in our religious or our secular schools — much interested in the subject. We don't honestly feel that there is any genuine need for so rarefied a pursuit. We cannot bring ourselves to believe that knowledge of the nature of art is possible or, if it is possible, that it is desirable. Yet we are engaged in a quarrel over the nature of art every day of our lives.

I do not see how we can hope to resolve that quarrel without making a sober and exhaustive effort to know what it is we are quarreling about. We cannot expect that a handful of dedicated men are going to starve to death while they do it for us; even if we were willing to let them starve and accomplish, it would take too long and make too small a dent. We cannot look to the educated minority — coming out of our colleges

— to conduct the necessary investigation and disseminate its findings unless the educated minority is, in fact, educated. We cannot hope for a popular acceptance of first principles until such time as a few first principles have been discovered or rediscovered and then articulated by men properly trained to use the proper tools.

We need knowledge desperately. We need two kinds: philosophical knowledge of the nature of art arrived at by the exercise of the human reason; and scientific knowledge of the effects of art arrived at by the accumulation of statistical data. I do not suppose that either will be easy to get. I do suppose that both can be got. I believe that it is the task of our universities to organize the search.

Unless we make the effort — on both sides and in good faith — we can only go on calling one another names, taking up sides out of simple instinct, and damaging the relationship between art and society by our excesses.

10

TENTATIVELY, and without an attempt to provide answers of my own, I should like to suggest one or two of the more hotly contended areas in which art might benefit — and so might criticism and censorship — by an attempt to define principle.

One of the most persistent fears tormenting the censorial mind is the fear that art is apt to stimulate in the audience the precise emotions that are described and developed in the art work. Lust on the stage is likely to beget lust out front; violence in a novel tends to produce violence on the street; and so on. Once our own emotions have been aroused by involvement in the fictitious emotions of others, there is no discharging them except in the conduct of our lives. The stimuli engendered by art have a carry-over value; we take them home with us, active and unfulfilled; they may become explosive at any time. The more powerful the art work the more powerful are its residual stimuli likely to be.

Since it is entirely characteristic of art that it should arouse powerful stimuli — that it should deal especially with those emotions that do drive men into active conflict — it is necessary to keep a watchful eye on *all* art. Art is, in its nature, risky; it is eternally playing with fire.

The science of aesthetics does have, however, a principle that might conceivably shed some light on the issue. It is called "catharsis," it makes its first appearance with Aristotle, and it is still remembered as a term though not regarded as an especially useful one.

When we speak of it today, we generally do so in terms of the latest psychological fashions; and we speak of it vaguely, at that. We have a hazy notion that Aristotle may have meant to suggest that the viewer's own life tensions were "purged" by the spectacle of tragedy; by the processes of identification and transfer, the tragic hero takes on something of our own burdens and expels them for us, or at least gives them a good shaking up. Perhaps we have a good many guilty impulses thrashing around inside us; perhaps we can see them objectified, realized, boldly acted upon by a character; perhaps this extension of our secret drives into mythical satisfaction gives us the feeling that we have been partially relieved of them, and so calms us down a bit. (The censorial mind automatically begins to wonder, at this point, if the spectator mayn't be sinning vicariously.) However we think of the term — and some criticism has chosen to dismiss the term, and the possible experience, as a fairly feeble form of sublimation, of little actual value or relevance to the essential working of art — we think of it in a "perhaps" fashion; it *may* mean something, but there isn't much chance of our pinning down that meaning with anything like precision, and even if there was it probably wouldn't be worth the labor. The term does not command our serious attention, certainly not in relation to our present conflict.

Since the problem of residual stimulus is one that no censor is ever going to dismiss lightly, and since "catharsis" at least sounds as though it might have some bearing on the problem, the term may be worth our serious attention. It may be worth our grass-roots attention, worth looking at in its simplest conceivable sense. What if, long before it plays any part in adjusting the personal and life-inspired emotions of the spectator, "catharsis" may be said to have some effect upon the emotions directly generated by the play?

Aristotle was engaged not in erecting some visionary standards toward a perfect play to be written in the future, but in reporting — and attempting to identify — certain real experiences he had observed taking place in the theater. It apparently came to his attention that spectators, on rising from their benches after a successfully worked-out play (and especially after a successfully worked-out tragedy), had a curious feeling of having been "cleansed." The feeling was an odd one, under the circumstances; why should a series of scenes in which characters act out of motives of lust, vengeance, and demonic pride end in the apparent purification, and relaxation, of the spectator? The audience has, in a sense, been urged to share Orestes' determination that his mother shall die; it has been literally terrified by the shocking descent of the Furies; it has watched Oedipus, his eyeballs torn out of their sockets, grope his way out of the palace that now houses the body of his suicide wife and mother. If the audience has to any degree participated in what

71

has gone forward, why doesn't it fly into the streets in a frenzy of despair?

There are, of course, a great many answers to this question, one lying within another and each striking deeper and deeper into the mysterious processes of art. For the moment let's talk about only the simplest and least sophisticated answer that might be given.

Suppose we grant at once that art does arouse certain stimuli in the spectator. It must, or it cannot hold him at all. The spectator must be caught by something: an arresting spot of color, an excitingly curved line, pity for an underdog, hatred for an obvious villain, a quick sympathy for young lovers. If the artist is to keep us attending to his work for its full duration, he must make us care — emotionally — whether or not Romeo wins Juliet, whether or not Hamlet exposes Claudius. The progression of involvement generally begins in the senses (so that attention may be swiftly seized), graduates to the emotions (so that attention may be sustained), and at last touches the intellect (so that attention may rest, at least intuitively, in what is intelligible). Every successful work of art will ask that the spectator commit himself — in some way and to some degree — sensually, emotionally, and intellectually. It does mean to *engage* his faculties.

And it might be helpful, along the way, if someone were to make a real effort to define the curious nature of this engagement. It is obviously not a full engagement; that is to say, we do not share Romeo's love for Juliet in the sense that we promptly fall in love with Juliet and want her for ourselves; we want her for Romeo, which is a quite different, and quite generous, emotion. Whatever we feel in the theater — or in any of our other experiences of art — is a third-party feeling; the feeling itself may become passionate, but the passion is — short of insanity — always the passion of an onlooker. We do not actually take over, lock, stock, and heavy breathing, the feelings of the party of the first part or the party of the second part.

But let's bypass for the moment — with the hope that this undefined relationship will sooner or later be subjected to serious study — the question of the *kind* of emotion generated in the spectator. *Some* kind of emotion does stir the spectator's blood stream; he is aroused, charged with stimuli, stirred up.

And the responses are multiple. The onlooker begins to adopt one emotional attitude toward Romeo, another toward Juliet, still another toward Tybalt. Each character, each described passion, each exciting situation brings its own stimulus. The spectator's emotions churn, move, surge ahead to some point of maximum intensity.

That point of maximum intensity is, of course, the climax of a play (in another art form, it might be that thrilling moment when we finally *see* the object whole). But a climax is, almost by definition, the point at which gathering forces, gathering stimuli, gathering emotions meet — and fuse. Everything that has been rushing forward now comes into violent collision. In the act of collision these things coalesce into an intelligible unity.

What makes them coalesce? The fusion at the point of climax comes because each powerful drive in the work finds, in the collision, its own satisfaction. In a painting a series of radically different, even opposed, colors, textures, and planes may be said to find a climactic harmony because they have been at last triumphantly related to one another; they come to rest in a harmony because they satisfy one another's needs. In a play, much more obviously, the hotly contending forces rise to a clash and, in the clash, complete themselves, exhaust their drives by successfully expelling their drives.

The restless stimulus of a vivid red may settle contentedly into a composition designed to embrace and to absorb it. Romeo's headlong passion for Juliet is "satisfied" not only by Romeo's possession of Juliet but by the death of Juliet. Hamlet's thirst for vengeance — or, if you will, justice — is satisfied by the destruction of Claudius. Whatever has kept the work thrashing vigorously forward now thrashes its last; the dynamic energy that has enthralled us is now a spent energy, subsiding into a coherent and conclusive pattern in which every passion finds its place.

Hamlet has felt a stimulus, has acted upon it, and has discharged it. If we have in some way shared the stimulus, we have in the same way shared its release, its self-satisfaction. Hamlet comes to rest, Claudius comes to rest, Gertrude comes to rest, vengeance itself comes to rest; so do we. A form of catharsis — perhaps a primitive one — has taken place. What the play has deliberately excited it has also deliberately discharged.

Indeed the final and chief pleasure of art, as has often been said, consists in the overwhelming coming together of so many disparate elements, in the establishment — or at least the unveiling — of an ultimate harmony. And the effect of this harmony upon us is peace, a profound sense of tranquillity, that familiar sensation of having been "cleansed." Art does not, in its nature, mean to send us away with a nagging burden of unfulfilled stimuli; its characteristic operation is one of fulfillment, of arriving at completion. St. Thomas, in a remark that may not have been sufficiently studied by the censorially minded, pointed out that "that belongs to the nature of the beautiful which, being seen or known, brings the appetite to rest." Beauty may, after all, be less a temptress than a tamer.

"Catharsis" may have much more value as a concept than is indicated here. Beyond suggesting that the sensations originated by art are also absorbed by art, it leads us toward all those more complex questions that ask how art affects sensations and emotions it does not originate, those that are brought, pre-formed and burdensome, into the arena by the spectator.

Our oversimplification may, however, indicate that study of the term is relevant to the very quarrels we are now engaged in. An attempt to define the concept — and it must be remembered that the concept is based on an actual experience of art — must surely prove profitable to critic and censor alike.

11

LET'S TENTATIVELY LOOK at another area of contention. We've already said that the average Catholic reviewer employs a double standard in forming and articulating his judgments. He makes one decision about the artistic quality of the work at hand, and another — perfectly isolated — decision about its moral character. He thereby places himself in the position of holding that a work of art may be good aesthetically, but unsound morally. He announces, in short, that a work may be both beautiful and bad.

The position is a queasy one. The reviewer is really only paying lip service to the secular critic in acknowledging the work's merit; his heart is not in the favorable portion of his verdict. And the secular critic, examining this verdict, becomes quickly convinced that the Catholic reviewer is unsympathetic to beauty itself, that he is willing to grind his heel on it whenever his nervous moral scruples are aroused.

The Catholic reviewer may have brought such distrust upon himself by failing to pay attention to certain of his own forebears. Thomas Aquinas did not leave us — possibly through the accidental loss of manuscripts — much of his thought on the subject of aesthetics. The most cursory examination of what he did leave behind him, though, quickly turns up a principle which Thomas calls "integrity." It is an aesthetic principle. In the Thomistic definition, a thing may be called beautiful when it is seen to possess integrity, proportion, and clarity.

"Integrity" in this context seems to mean wholeness or completeness. That is to say, the object at hand is in full possession of all its necessary parts; nothing essential to the object is lacking, nothing irrelevant to the object is present. Nature is the source of the art object; when a man makes an imitation of nature, "integrity" requires that his imitation be wholly accurate. He must not wantonly subtract from what *is;* he must not willfully add to it. His work will be beautiful when it respects the existential "truth" of things so thoroughly that that truth is rendered with utter fidelity. The artist tries to mirror essential being precisely. (The artist may never achieve his goal absolutely; but his work becomes beautiful in proportion as it seizes the fullness — unencumbered by excrescence — of its source in nature.)

Now whenever the Catholic reviewer finds himself quarreling with the "moral" character of a work, he generally means to say that something has been added to nature (perhaps a certain action has been given a sentimental coloration that it does not in fact possess) or that something has been subtracted from nature (perhaps a certain action has not been given all the effects that are proper to it). An image has either been unsuitably adorned or unhappily truncated.

Suppose that a work does contain a sentimental overlay, or that it lacks one of its essential members. (It has not told the whole truth; it has slopped over or it has stopped short.) If it is deficient in integrity, and if integrity is a valid aesthetic requirement, it now becomes impossible to describe the work as aesthetically fine but morally corrupt. The question of moral corruptness — an ambiguous one at best, since neither the heart of the artist nor the response of the spectator can be perfectly known — does not even come up. The work is *aesthetically* defective, not a good work of art. The double standard disappears. A work cannot be "morally corrupt" (I am trying to use the phrase here as I think the

Catholic reviewer uses it, to indicate a serious excrescence or a serious omission) and still be beautiful; conversely, a work cannot be genuinely beautiful (possessed of integrity, wholeness, fidelity) and be "morally corrupt." A thing cannot be true and not true at one and the same time.

If the disturbing double standard disappears, though, it disappears because we have for the moment abandoned our attempt to come at a judgment "morally" — by laboriously guessing at the effect a work is likely to have on its audience — and have tried to evaluate an aesthetic object with aesthetic tools. We have asked the question: is the work complete, does it satisfy — without gratuitous addition or subtraction — its own requirements? The shift in footing may bring certain interesting results: it may suggest to critic and censor alike that there is never any real clash between good art and good morals; it may suggest to both the moralist and the artist that, while they are moving toward truth by different routes, they are moving toward the same truth; it may, by giving the Catholic reviewer his proper equipment, also give him the courage to say what is in his mind (he has actually been weaseling); and it may, by defining an aesthetic principle and using the principle to reach an aesthetic verdict, reopen the conversation with secular criticism on mutually intelligible grounds. This last point might well be stressed. The secular critic now has a chance of knowing what the Catholic critic is talking about, and the Catholic critic will no longer be talking double talk. Both will be speaking the same language: the language demanded by the object under discussion. The secular critic and the Catholic critic may still, on certain occasions, disagree; each may challenge the other's accurate use of aesthetic tools. But because both are making use of a principle that can be defined, and because both have a stake in the vigorous assertion of the principle itself, the door to agreement is at least — and at last — open.

12

SINCE WE ARE obviously standing on the threshold of an ideal world here, let's brashly step inside it for a moment. Let's say that we have all developed our critical faculties and our critical tools to the point where we feel confident that we are moving toward art with the *right* tools. Let's say that we know enough about the workings of art to move toward it with an easy affection, secure in our feeling that good art and a good society can be produced at one and the same time. Let's suppose that, if the truly authorized censor is still lodged in his office, his function has been defined as an extraordinary one. In the ordinary course of affairs we are devoting our energies — confidently, affectionately, and efficiently — to answering the question: is this a good or a bad work of *art?*

Finding it a good one, we shall now feel free to relax with it. Finding it a bad one, we can throw it away with a light heart — letting the censor catch it if he wants to.

The truth of the matter is that none of us — not even the most passionate opponent of the very principle of censorship — really cares what happens to bad art. If the work is aesthetically poor, we don't honestly care what the censor does with it, or what anyone else does with it. The world can wrap fish with it — as it most certainly will — and we're not going to mind.

The essential fear that nags at the critical mind whenever it is confronted by censorship is the fear that *good* art will be lost. This is a valid, reasonable fear. The possibility is a real possibility. There is the further fear, and the further possibility, that in an atmosphere dominated by widespread, habitual, amateur censorship good art will never even be produced, let alone lost. This fear can only be quieted by an agreement on both sides that the due aesthetic judgment be made first; arrangements for the suitable disposal of what turns out to be worthless work can be made later.

There is a continuing fear nagging at the censorial mind, too. It is the fear that, no matter what aesthetic principles are evolved and agreed upon, no matter how "safe" good art may prove to be, bad art will still be produced — and circulated. If it should be shown, for instance, that successful work absorbs its own stimuli, what about the stimuli generated by unsuccessful work? If it is true that a genuinely beautiful work is, by virtue of its integrity, also a genuinely "moral" work, what about the effect of work that lacks integrity, is not beautiful, is only meretriciously but perhaps persuasively "pretty"?

Again, there is only one way of working toward an answer. It must first be decided what the work *is*, in its own nature. Stimuli are engendered in both good and bad art, very often the same stimuli. The only way the moralist can come to know whether these stimuli are discharged within the work or allowed to seethe, unfulfilled, long after, is by examining the aesthetic character of the work. He must know how art operates in general, and how each individual work of art operates in particular.

I think there is no resolving our present dilemma, no escaping the increasing tensions of a tug-of-war in which both parties are committed to unalterable positions, except by the rational development of a demonstrable, defensible aesthetic.

13

IF ANSWERS are possible, they are still a long way off. The work involved in seeking them is obviously tremendous. Is the ideal world — in which we know at least some of the answers — so distant that we really cannot count on arriving at it in any practical sense? Is the work involved so tremendous that we cannot hope to see it done? Aren't we better off pursuing our present compromises, and even our present prejudices, than risking the further corruption of society while we put our noses into books and our energies into splitting hairs?

The censorial attitude is, of course, principally concerned with the health of society. Its various acts are performed in the interests of sanity, balance, all those qualities that help keep the moral life of the community on an even keel.

But the health of society, it must be remembered, does not come from negative, protective acts alone. Caution in itself does not guarantee a man safe and sound passage through a complex world. The constitution of a society is not necessarily made strong by *not* doing things.

Health is as much the result of positive, vigorously creative acts as it is of prudential acts; joyous absorption in work going forward may even be healthier than a timorous refusal to expose oneself to possible dangers. Hypochondria is in itself an illness.

It was in speaking, briefly, of the theater that St. Thomas said: "The object of play-acting is to cheer the heart of man. Play is necessary for the intercourse of human life. No man can exist without pleasure, and when he cannot enjoy the pleasures of the spirit he seeks those of the flesh."

We might do very well, in our present state of nerves, to underscore certain of St. Thomas' words. Play is *necessary* to healthful human life. The man who has learned to avoid it, to distrust it, to indulge it rarely and then in apprehension, is well on his way toward being something a great deal less than a whole man. If he is, out of good enough motives, going to deny himself something essential to his existence he is going to get both himself and his society into immediate trouble. He is going to destroy his own objectives: balance, sanity, mental and moral fitness.

No man can *exist* without pleasure; the Puritan shrivels within himself and loses a part of his very being. A society committed to a Puritan habit of thought, or even a semi-Puritan habit of thought, is not a living society but a half-fossilized one. And within the Puritan core strange new excesses will begin to appear. "When he cannot enjoy the pleasures of the spirit he seeks those of the flesh."

It would seem to be St. Thomas' view, then, that art is not a temptation roughly equivalent to the temptations of the flesh. It is, on the contrary, an indispensable antidote to the pleasures of the flesh, a spiritual satisfaction that diminishes rather than intensifies the fleshly appetites. Even this is too negative a way of putting it. Art viewed as an antidote alone is art grudgingly admitted to the social scene. Art is, quite simply, a spiritual food essential to the human diet. It is not medication for a disease incurred elsewhere; it is a natural staple whose neglect will bring on disease and ultimately demand medication.

If we are to take St. Thomas' words seriously, we are bound to acknowledge that a lively, cheerful, openhearted interest in art is a clear prerequisite for personal and social health. It is, it turns out, perfectly possible for a society to be prudently, scrupulously self-protective — and still be sick. Bundling up won't do the job all by itself; exercise is essential. As Catholics, we've been doing a lot of bundling up and taking very little exercise. American society as a whole is not, at the moment, in very trim shape. If we have, or are on the way to having, a society that is partially sick, it is because very few of us have learned how to be properly playful.

The diffusion of the censorial mind over the whole community is, to be blunt about it, a sign of sickness. I think that the hysterical refusal of the critical and censorial camps to attempt any sort of mediation is a further sign of fundamental disbalance, an unrealistic clinging to indefensible extremes.

The defender of art and the defender of prudence are actually interested in the same objectives, in slightly different proportions. Each really wants good art, though neither has as yet been careful to make explicit his idea of good art. Each really wants a good society, though neither has as yet attempted to explain to the other his concept of art's function in creating the good society.

It will be necessary, I think, to undertake the long labor of making meanings explicit — of defining terms, of developing rational demonstrations, of accumulating clear evidence, of constructing in the end a philosophy of art — if these two belligerents are ever to see what astonishing things they have in common.

At present we simply do not know enough to be able to shake hands on anything. Our ignorance is not a hopeless ignorance, though. The things we *need* to know are pretty plainly marked out, indicated by the particular quarrels we are engaged in. It is clearly time for all of us — and in particular the universities, secular and religious — to establish machinery for the pursuit of the peculiar knowledge we need, and to set that machinery in motion.

CRITICISM AND CENSORSHIP

By Walter Kerr

CAN there be a meeting of minds between the critic passionately dedicated to the arts and the censor worried about their possible indiscretions and harmful effects? Is censorship of movies, books, and plays justified? If so, how far should it extend and what are the conditions for its legitimate exercise? To modern Americans these questions pose problems of vital, burning importance; yet their solution is admittedly difficult.

Criticism and Censorship, an expanded version of the fifth lecture in the Gabriel Richard Series, delivered at St. Louis University in 1954, is an articulate attempt at an answer to the complicated issue of censorship. As such it is a worthy addition to the lectures named in honor of the pioneering Sulpician priest, teacher, and patriot, Gabriel Richard of Detroit.

Mr. Kerr, drama critic for the *New York Herald-Tribune,* first notes the mounting tension over the problem. The critic, in his enthusiasm for the arts, thirsts for the complete defeat of the principle of censorship as such, viewing it as an unwarranted foray into the realm of human liberty. The forces of censorship, aware that they are losing ground in the courts, have turned to the formation of powerful pressure groups whose weapons today are not so much philosophical or legal as economic.

This tension is especially stormy among present-day Catholics. In general, the Catholic critic, to resolve the tension between the